Y0-BRF-714

The Brooklyn Bridge

SRA

Columbus, OH

SRAonline.com

 SRA

Send all inquiries to this address:
SRA/McGraw-Hill
4400 Easton Commons
Columbus, OH 43219

ISBN: 978-0-07-608709-9
MHID: 0-07-608709-3

1 2 3 4 5 6 7 8 9 NOR 13 12 11 10 09 08 07

The Brooklyn Bridge is more than just a bridge. It is a structure that changed the face of the United States after the Civil War. The bridge connected Brooklyn and New York City, but its impact was far-reaching.

Building the bridge was an amazing achievement. It was possible because of new technology. It took fourteen years to build. It opened in 1883.

The bridge was a symbol of progress, invention, hope, and possibility. It showed what people were capable of creating. It reflected the growth of the country as a whole. Since it was built, it has inspired artists, writers, poets, and photographers.

About the Bridge

The Brooklyn Bridge is more than one hundred years old. The number of people in New York City has grown greatly since it first opened. Yet the bridge is still important to the public and the city. Each day about 145,000 vehicles cross the bridge. In addition, thousands of people walk across it.

The bottom part of the bridge is for cars and trucks. The top part of the bridge has a wide road that is open to people walking or riding bikes. When it was first built, trains crossed the bridge. However, the train tracks were removed about sixty years ago.

The Brooklyn Bridge crosses the East River. The part of the bridge that hangs over the river is 1,595 feet long. That is about as long as five football fields. The total length of the bridge is almost six thousand feet, which is more than one mile long. Four main steel cables hang across the river. The roadway hangs from these cables. Each roadway has 3,515 miles of wire in it!

Two hundred and eight smaller cables hang down from the main cables. They add extra support. The bridge has two massive towers. They rise 276 feet above the water. They support most of the road's weight.

Effects of the Bridge

When it was built, the Brooklyn Bridge joined two of the country's largest cities of the time, Brooklyn and New York City. The bridge made travel between the two cities much easier. Before the bridge was built, people had to cross the river by ferryboat. The ferryboats were often delayed due to tides or the weather. The bridge, however, could be crossed at any time.

The bridge also allowed New York City to continue to grow. Many people moved to the less crowded Brooklyn and then crossed the bridge to go to work in New York.

The bridge led to a greater interest and trust in technology. One example of a new technology used to build the bridge was the use of steel. Steel was very strong and inexpensive compared to other metals available at that time.

Throughout construction, new machines were brought in to help the laborers who built the bridge. In fact, new machines made the building of the bridge possible in the first place. Many of these machines were steam-powered. The cranes that lifted and moved heavy material were steam-powered. Steel drills were used to break up rock.

The building of the Brooklyn Bridge occurred at the same time as corporations were arising in the United States. A corporation is an organization set up to conduct business.

In 1866 the state of New York passed a bill. It called for the construction of a bridge across the East River.

The next year New York Bridge Company was set up. It was a corporation with a board of directors. It was a business that set in motion the building of the East River bridge. That bridge eventually became the Brooklyn Bridge.

The success of the Brooklyn Bridge led to the building of other bridges. In New York three other bridges were built after the turn of the century. In addition, a number of tunnels were built. This was partly because the bridge introduced new technology. It opened people's minds to new possibilities in building.

Fifteen years after the bridge opened, Brooklyn became part of New York City. Today New York City is the largest city in the United States. The bridge helped it thrive and grow into the city it is today.

Building the Bridge

The person who designed the Brooklyn Bridge was John Roebling. He began thinking about the bridge after he got stuck on the river while crossing by ferryboat. That was in 1857. Ten years later he was named chief engineer of the project.

Like many of the people who worked on building the Brooklyn Bridge, Roebling was an immigrant. He came to the United States in 1831 from Germany. He worked hard, and he became rich from a wire cable business he started. Wire cable was much stronger than other ropes being used at that time. It was used instead of rope in large construction projects.

Roebling worked out a detailed plan for the Brooklyn Bridge. But many people did not think Roebling's plan was possible. No other bridge spanned a distance as great as the distance across the East River. In fact, at that time, about one out of every four bridges collapsed soon after being built!

Crowded waters around Manhattan in 1875

Shortly before construction began, a boat crushed Roebling's foot. He developed a disease as a result of the injury. Soon after that he died. Some people thought this meant the bridge would not be built. However, Roebling's son, Washington, took over for his father.

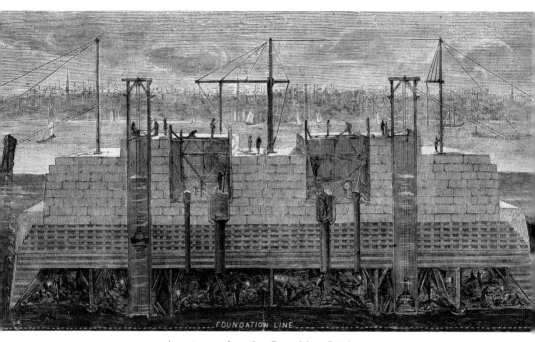

A caisson for the Brooklyn Bridge

Many problems came up after construction began. The first part of the bridge that was built were *caissons*. These are large, watertight boxes. They were placed in the river so that the towers could be built on top of them. The caissons were the largest ones ever built. They could hold four tennis courts each. After they were sunk in the river, compressed air was forced into them. This air is different from the air that we normally breathe. Little was known about it during the building of the bridge. It hurt and even killed many of the men who worked in the caissons.

The gases in this air made some of the workers sick with another illness. The bends is a type of sickness that deep-sea divers sometimes get. It occurs when the pressure of compressed air is released too quickly. When this happens, gas bubbles from the compressed air are released into the bloodstream. This causes severe pain in one's joints. The illness got its name because the people who are affected cannot stand or walk upright. Some of the workers died from this sickness. One of the men affected with the bends was Roebling. By the end of 1872, he could no longer work on site.

Inside a caisson

Roebling was forced to direct the building of the bridge from his home. He could watch the work from his window by using binoculars. He tried to find new solutions to the problems workers faced.

Roebling wrote detailed instructions. That way the laborers who worked on the project would know what to do. But the work inside the caissons became even more dangerous. The workers began using dynamite in the chambers. This was done to break apart the large rocks on the bottom of the river so that the caissons could sit on an even surface.

After the caissons were completed, the towers were built on top of them. Each tower took four years to build. The towers were made of a type of rock called granite.

At the time they were built, they were taller than any other building in the country. People did not have the knowledge and tools to build very tall structures. Roebling helped change that. Many tons of stone were used to build the massive towers.

The bridge became a huge structure that towered over the tallest buildings in the busy city, the tallest of which was only five stories.

Brooklyn Bridge tower

15

Anchorages made the bridge stable. They were built after the towers. Located at the far ends of the bridge, they were almost ninety feet tall. They were more than one hundred feet long and wide.

With the giant structures in place, the first cable was strung in 1876. The cable was about as thick as a person's thumb.

A seat was made out of a board and attached to the wire. One of the longtime bridge workers rode across the river on it. It was a historic journey, and ten thousand people gathered to watch.

Master Mechanic E. F. Farrington was the worker who made the journey. He climbed the eighty-foot tower on the Brooklyn side and sat on the seat. An engine was connected to the cable. He was then pulled across the river by the engine.

Farrington's ride symbolized the joining of the two cities. It also proved the strength of the cable. The workers would soon be attached to the cables as they worked on the roadway. Farrington's ride made the workers feel safer about this new danger they faced.

A Suspension Bridge

The Brooklyn Bridge was designed as a suspension bridge. This kind of bridge uses cables that are suspended, or hung, over the obstacle to be crossed. The cables are strung through two towers. The towers stand at either end of the bridge. The cables form an "M" shape. The two high points of the letter sit on top of the two towers. The roadway hangs from the cables. It is attached to the top cables by other smaller, vertical cables. The towers support most of the road's weight.

There are many different types of bridges. Suspension bridges have advantages over some of the others. One of the advantages is that a suspension bridge can span a great distance with the use of only two towers, one at either end. It does not have to have extra towers in the middle. Another advantage of a suspension bridge is that its construction uses less material than many other types of bridges.

Immigrants' Contributions

Great contributions were made by immigrants during the building of the bridge. John Roebling, the man who dreamed of, designed, and began the bridge was a German immigrant. He moved to the United States when he was twenty-five years old to be a farmer. He got tired of this and decided to go back to engineering, which was what he had studied at school.

Many of the laborers who actually built the bridge were immigrants as well. Many of them had come to the United States from Germany, Ireland, and Italy. The assistance they provided was invaluable. Without them, the bridge would not have been built.

The work was long and hard. It was often dangerous. Surprisingly, there were not numerous strikes during the construction. There was only one time that the laborers stopped working as a form of protest. After men who worked in the caissons began dying of the bends, the other workers dreaded going under the water. They were afraid they, too, might become sick and die. They wanted higher wages to make up for the risks they had to take while working. They left their jobs for three days. After they were told they would all be fired if they did not return, they went back to work.

Celebration

After fourteen years and more than fifteen million dollars, the Brooklyn Bridge was finished. President Chester Arthur attended the ceremony. He led a large group of people across the bridge on this important occasion. During the celebration, about fourteen tons of fireworks exploded over the bridge. Hundreds of thousands of people attended. More than 150,000 people walked across the bridge that day. However, Washington Roebling was not one of them. Still weak from his illness and from the stress of his work, he never set foot on his creation.

Other Technological Advances

During the time that the Brooklyn Bridge was built, many other exciting changes were taking place in the United States. In 1869 the first transcontinental railroad was completed, stretching from one side of the country to the other.

Barbed wire was invented in the 1860s. The first practical machine for its manufacture was invented in 1874. By 1890 the open range of the western United States had become fenced pastureland.

In 1876 Alexander Graham Bell invented the telephone. One year later Thomas Edison invented the phonograph, or record player. In 1880 Edison invented the lightbulb. And in 1883 the first skyscraper was built in Chicago. It was ten stories high!

Vocabulary

laborers (lā´ bûr ûrz) (page 7) *n.* Plural form of **laborer:** A worker.

thrive (thrīv) (page 9) *v.* To succeed; to grow well.

binoculars (bə no´ kyə lûrz) (page 14) *n.* A tool for seeing far away, made of two telescopes joined together to allow the viewer to use both eyes.

strikes (strīks) (page 21) *n.* Plural form of **strike:** A work stoppage as a form of protest.

dreaded (dre´ dəd) (page 21) *v.* Past tense of **dread:** To fear.

wages (wā´ jəz) (page 21) *n.* Plural form of **wage:** Pay received for work.

Comprehension Focus: Visualize

1. Describe how you visualized an event in the story.

2. Describe how you visualize the crossing of the East River before and after the construction of the Brooklyn Bridge.